The Mystery of Human Suffering

OR

The Chastenings of the Lord

First Fruits Press
The Academic Open Press of Asbury Theological Seminary
204 N. Lexington Ave., Wilmore, KY 40390
859-858-2236
first.fruits@asburyseminary.edu
asbury.to/firstfruits

THE MYSTERY OF HUMAN SUFFERING
OR
THE CHASTENINGS OF THE LORD

Commencement Sermon at
Asbury College
May 31, 1931

by
Rev. H. C. Morrison, D. D.

First Fruits Press
Wilmore, KY
2015

The Mystery of Human Suffering; or, The Chastenings of the Lord

Published by First Fruits Press, © 2015
Digital version at
http://place.asburyseminary.edu/firstfruitsheritagematerial/85/

ISBN: 9781621711667 (print), 9781621711674 (digital),
9781621711681 (kindle)

Morrison, H. C. (Henry Clay), 1857-1942.
    The mystery of human suffering, or, The chastenings of the Lord :
    commencement sermon at Asbury College, May 31, 1931 / by H.C.
    Morrison.
    The chastenings of the Lord.
    20 pages ; 21 cm.
    Wilmore, Ky. : First Fruits Press, c2014.
    Reprint. Previously published: Louisville, KY : Pentecostal Publishing
    Company, [1931].
    ISBN: 9781621711667(pbk.)
    1. Bible. Hebrews XII, 9-10 -- Sermons. 2. Baccalaureate addresses –
    Asbury College (Wilmore, Ky.) 3. Sermons ,American. I. Title.
    BV4255 .M6 2014

Cover by Haley Hill

CONTENTS

· · · · · · · · · · ·

PREFACE

· · · · · · · · · · ·

    Dr. Akers, President of Asbury College, asked me to preach the Commencement Sermon at the close of its forty-second year. I hardly felt able for the task; when I went into the great Hughes' Auditorium and saw the vast audience, I got an inspiration that greatly strengthened my body. The prayer and song thrilled my soul. I had a few notes, but forgot to notice them. Many of my friends insisted that the sermon should be printed. I have written it the best I can, from memory. I trust it may prove a blessing to many of the Lord's chastened children.

Faithfully yours,
H. C. Morrison

INTRODUCTION

· · · · · · · · · · ·

It was my privilege and joy to hear this sermon preached in the Auditorium, chaste and beautiful as a Greek temple, at Asbury College, and with others, I urged its publication.

The weather was hot. Dr. Morrison was not well. The weight of years oppressed him. The snows of seventy-four winters were on his head. He sat erect, but wearily, surrounded by younger men in the prime of life. Before him was a great and expectant audience. Behind him was the noble organ and the massed student choir. The organ trumpeted and pealed forth its ocean-toned diapason. The great choir sang the Hallelujah Chorus. The unseen hosts of God seemed hovering over and all around about us. Every heart was stirred.

Fire of the Holy Ghost kindled and flamed in Dr. Morrison. Weariness slipped off him. He was a young man once more. His step was nimble, his voice was vibrant, his thought was luminous. His speech flowed in a torrent. His soul flashed fire. The audience responded with tears, with laughter, with fervent amens, and I doubt not with renewed faith and deepened consecration, not only to do, but to suffer gladly all the will of God.

His purpose in Christ to make us a holy people, partakers of the Divine nature, and his use of the chastenings and amazements and perplexities and agonies of life in working out this end never looked so gracious and kindly, and we were confirmed in our deepest convictions that the sable-clad messenger bearing life's woes and sorrows, when stripped of their black masks will reveal shining faces that have looked upon the face of God, and that whatever may befall us, God means us no harm, but only good, if we but nestle down into his will and believe.

I know from experience how next to impossible it is for a preacher to recover from a few notes a sermon, delivered before a responsive and eager audience under special inspiration, but I rejoice that Dr. Morrison has succeeded so well, and I trust this sermon may receive the wide and permanent circulation it deserves.

S. L. Brengle,
Commissioner

MYSTERY OF HUMAN SUFFERING

• • • • • • • • • •

"We have had fathers after our flesh which
corrected us, and we gave them reverence:
shall we not much rather be in subjection
unto the Father of spirits, and live? For
they verily for a few days chastened us
after their own pleasure; but he for our
profit, that we might be partakers of his
holiness." Hebrews 12 :9-10

The mystery of human suffering is one of the
most profound and difficult problems that can claim
our attention. It is a problem which, sooner or later,
confronts all of us. Suffering physical, mental, and
spiritual insists upon a place in the program of the life
of every individual. Who has not, in times of extreme
suffering, or deep sorrow, been made to cry out, "Why is
this? Why should I be called upon to pass through such
an ordeal of agony?" Philosophers have failed to give a

satisfactory explanation of human suffering. They have found no panacea for our pains. Our text sheds a flood of light on this subject. Let us give it careful study.

The Epistle to the Hebrews was written by a Hebrew. It was a splendid effort of an inspired apostle to convince the Hebrew people that Jesus of Nazareth, whom they had crucified, was the promised Messiah of Old Testament prophecy. He begins by showing his people that Jesus was superior to all men, superior to all priests, and high above all angels; that he is one, and equal with God; that, in his crucifixion, a way was provided for the redemption of men from sin.

There has been quite a bit of discussion with reference to the authorship of the Epistle to the Hebrews. It is said to be the most eloquently written book in the Bible, Old Testament or New. Some have suggested that it was probably written by the eloquent Apollos. We believe the best scholarship recognizes St. Paul as the author of this great Epistle. The fact of its eloquence is by no means proof that it is not the product of the inspired mind of Paul. Paul's speech before Agrippa has been regarded as a masterpiece. To be deeply in love with a great subject, to be mastered by a passion for a people and a purpose, to be well informed with regard to the facts that concern the welfare, uplift, and salvation of a people, furnishes a man with conditions and inspiration that may easily produce eloquence.

St. Paul was deeply in love with Israel; not only with the tenacious affection of an Israelite, but a divine love had been shed abroad within him; it had lifted him in to sacred heights of intense longing for their enlightenment and salvation by faith in the Christ they had rejected and crucified. He reached the highest altitudes of unselfish solicitude, when he cried out. "I could wish that myself were accursed from Christ for my brethren, my kinsmen according to the flesh."

We have been interested to notice the strong resemblance between Moses and St. Paul. They were both intense, unselfish lovers of their people. This has been characteristic of the Hebrews from the days of Abraham to the present. You remember that when Moses came down from the mount and found his people in indolatry, and God proposed to destroy the people and make Moses the fountainhead of a great nation, Moses cried out, "Yet now, if thou wilt forgive their sin; and if not, blot me, I pray thee, out of thy book which thou hast written."

Such love and solicitude, with the material at his command, and all set ablaze by the Holy Spirit, fully prepared the Apostle Paul for the mountain peaks of eloquence found in the Epistle to the Hebrews. The eleventh chapter of the Epistle to the Hebrews has been called the "Hall of Fame of the saints." It is a grand gallery of pictures of heroic souls drawn true to life by inspired hands. As we walk down the aisles of this gallery we find

Abel, with his acceptable offering; Enoch, walking away to heaven with God; Noah, building an ark of safety for his family; Abraham, going out without knowing whither he went; Isaac and Jacob dwelling in tabernacles; Sarah conceiving a wonderful child in her old age; Joseph, in his integrity and purity of heart, now in prison, then ruling in Egypt. We find Israel marching through the Red Sea on dry land. Faith is the invisible battering ram that breaks down the walls of Jericho. Rahab, of a strange people, saves herself and family by faith. A great army of holy men and women come crowding into the mind of the Apostle, and he enumerates the names of mighty souls who, by faith, subdued kingdoms, wrought righteousness, and obtained promises, stopped the mouths of lions, quenched the violence of fire, escaped the edge of the sword, out of weakness were made strong, waxed valiant in fight, turned to flight the armies of the aliens. Women received their dead raised to life again: others were tortured, not accepting deliverance; that they might obtain a better resurrection: others had trials of cruel mockings and scourgings, yea, moreover of bonds and imprisonment: they were stoned, they were sawn asunder, were tempted, were slain with the sword; they wandered about in sheepskins and goatskins; being destitute, afflicted, tormented; of whom the world was not worthy: they wandered in deserts, and in mountains, and in dens and caves of the earth. And these all, obtained a good report through faith.

The inspired writer tells us that they did all this without receiving the fulfillment of the promise. Jesus had not yet come in the flesh. The contract had been let for the erection of a redemptive bridge spanning the chasm of sin and death and hell, but the structure had not been erected. These mighty souls were so full of faith, they so restfully and perfectly believed in God and his word, that they were lifted up into the reality of things. They could walk on promises, and they strode across in triumph where the bridge was to be built.

The inspired writer is seeking to show his people in the times of persecution and intense suffering, the power of faith; how that there is a mighty God who is able to meet every difficulty, and to give his people deliverance out of their sufferings, or patience to endure them without murmuring. Let us not forget that this record of the victories of faith is for us today; that we are living in a world of sin; that if we would be separated from its sinful ways, we may expect its contempt and opposition, and we shall need to so ally ourselves, by faith, with the great God of the universe that, whatever comes, we may be assured of his presence to deliver and keep in peace in times of deepest and most mysterious agony.

I have sometimes thought that the record given us of Job, with his afflictions, and the man who was born blind, whom Jesus healed, gives us a sort of multiplication table by which we can figure out the meaning of human suffering. Job did not suffer because of sin, but Satan set upon him because of his perfections of character. In his sufferings, however, he learned deeper and higher lessons than could have otherwise come to him.

Here is a babe born blind. The parents cannot understand. No doubt the neighbors whisper among themselves that it is a judgment sent upon them. The blind boy suffers his disadvantages, grows into a man, and wonders why he is so sorely afflicted. But Jesus passed by and healed him. The disciples, in their stupidity, associate this affliction with sin, and ask the clumsy question, "Master, who did sin, this man, or his parents, that he was born blind?" Jesus answers, "Neither hath this man sinned, nor his parents: but that the works of God should be made manifest in him." It seems to me that this throws a flood of light on this problem of human suffering. We have men suffering, not because of sin, but for the revelation of divine truth.

We may read the Bible and, in a way, believe it. We may have great desire, good motives, and intentions. We may pray and weep, and long and fail, but if we will add faith, unhesitating faith, in God, his power, his promises, and his love, the trees of difficulty will be plucked up by the roots and flung into the sea, where they disappear, and go down so deep that they can never block the traffic of faith, or interfere with the commerce of love and blessing between heaven and earth. The mountains that lift their lofty peaks in the way of our spiritual progress and service can be easily removed by the mighty scoop shovel of faith in God. Jesus Christ has said, "All things are possible to him that believeth." When this epistle was written it cost something to be a Christian. There were oppositions, tests, and persecutions. The inspired writer is seeking to comfort and encourage the people by surrounding them with a cloud of witnesses who have believed in the Christ of promise, who had not as yet appeared. The people to whom he wrote had better things. Christ had appeared, lived, loved, and taught; had been crucified, had arisen from the dead, and had been revealed to them by the Holy Spirit.

In all that the apostle has said in the eleventh and twelfth chapters of this epistle, he is paving the way to the high altitudes where we find our text. The text is an open door into this profound philosophy of human sorrow and suffering. It is not an accident; it is the divine discipline. It is not to gratify the whim of an almighty tyrant; it is the chastening of a compassionate Father. It is a part of the program that must be expected and gracefully submitted to by every child of God. The apostle assures us that no one of us can expect to be exempt from the chastening rod. It is the divine tribulum that separates the good wheat of holiness from the straw and chaff of carnality.

My dear young friends, I am profoundly interested in you, in your future, in the building of your character, in your loyalty to your Christ and your service to your fellow beings. My good wishes and prayers will follow you. I am especially concerned about your sorrows; the oppositions and difficulties with which you are to meet. I am thinking with profound solicitude, of the chastenings that await you, and how you will meet them, whether in the spirit of rebellion, or meekness and submission.

The apostle readily admits that, "No chastening for the present seemeth to be joyous, but grievous: nevertheless afterward it yieldeth the peaceable fruits of righteousness unto them which are exercised thereby." May God grant you wisdom and grace to so endure the compassionate chastenings of the Lord, that they shall bring you the peaceable fruits of righteousness.

It is a blessed consolation to understand that there is nothing haphazard in the life of the child of God, but that there is a divine order, and that God has for us the highest possible purpose; that he is striving to bring us to partake of his holiness. What a thought! It bows us in humility. It thrills us with an inspiring hope. It lifts us into the high altitudes of the wondrous redemption wrought by Christ, and the infinite purpose of the great God who built the illimitable universe, and leads us by the gracious hand of his power, correcting, rebuking, instructing and even, inflicting agony of body, mind, and spirit, that he may bring us into that submissiveness of our will, that panting after God, like the hart for the waterbrook, that will enable him to pour into us his own holiness.

The text contains a great breaking of daylight upon us; in fact, of heavenly light. In the text, the Sun of righteousness breaks through all the clouds of our human sorrow with healing in his wings; and so we take the path of life with our small, weak hands in the mighty hand that fashioned the spheres, to lead us on through whatever comes, up into the celestial heights of his holiness.

Peter tells us that we may be "made partakers of the divine nature." The Apostle Paul assures us that "the love of God is shed abroad in our hearts by the Holy Ghost being given unto us." "The love of God," mark you! The love with which God loves a lost world. The love that gave an only Son to redeem a lost and sinful world. A love that enables us to love, to forgive, to labor, to suffer, and to wait submitted to the divine will, enraptured in blessed fellowship with the Holy Trinity. With this text shedding its illumination upon us, we are better prepared to meet the vicissitudes of life.

We have been interested to watch the builder, with the blueprints of the architect, lay his foundation, lift his majestic walls, and ornament his structure with arches, columns, and naves. God is both the architect and builder of human character. The prints are not made in blue, but they are traced out with the red blood of the cross. This infinite Architect knows exactly what his objective is, and understands each stroke in order to bring his purpose to its glorious completion. He wants to solve the whole sin problem. He wants to bring us into harmony with himself. His great desire is that we shall hate what he hates, and love what he loves. He would make us Godlike. He will work away until we shall gladly bear the reproach of Christ, who went without the gates of the ancient city of Jerusalem, to suffer the agonies of the cross, that he might sanctify the people with his own blood. The Architect who is at work building our character, will not, cannot, be satisfied until we are perfected in love; until all stain of sin disappears; until we can be presented before the Father in the midst of assembled angels and saints, without spot or wrinkle.

I delight to watch the artist. I see him paint his background, and then the picture he has visioned with his mind's eye begins to take form. We are mystified at first, but gradually, we see his thought appearing upon the canvas, and on he goes with delicate, meaningful touch here and there, until the picture seems to live and breathe. Our heavenly Father is the Artist working upon our immortal spirits, who will not be satisfied until we are presented to the highest intelligences of the universe in the beauty of holiness.

My mind is enraptured. My soul is uplifted. I gaze with wonder and delight into the profound meaning of our sorrows and sufferings. Our heavenly Father is with us, laboring, loving, chastening, lifting, until he can bring us into such rapturous submission and unquestioning faith that he can impart to us his own holiness.

I can say no more. My message is delivered. My heart is on fire. My faith lays hold upon the Lamb of God whose precious blood cleanseth us from all sin. Let me quote the text: "We have had fathers after our flesh which corrected us, and we gave them reverence; shall we not much rather be in subjection unto the Father of spirits, and live? For they verily for a few days chastened us after their own pleasure; but he for our profit, that we might be partakers of his holiness."